Chicago

A PHOTOGRAPHIC PORTRAIT

PHOTOGRAPHY BY DON BROWN

First published in the United States
of America by:

Twin Lights Publishers, Inc.
8 Hale Street
Rockport, Massachusetts 01966
Telephone: (978) 546-7398
http://www.twinlightspub.com

ISBN-13: 978-1-885435-57-6
ISBN-10: 1-885435-57-6

10 9 8 7 6 5 4 3

Editorial researched and written by:
Francesca Yates and Duncan Yates

Book design by
SYP Design & Production, Inc.
http://www.sypdesign.com

Printed in China

Introduction

"We struck the home trail now, and in a few hours were in that astonishing Chicago—a city where they are always rubbing a lamp, and fetching up the genii, and contriving and achieving new impossibilities. It is hopeless for the occasional visitor to try to keep up with Chicago—she outgrows her prophecies faster than she can make them. She is always a novelty; for she is never the Chicago you saw when you passed through the last time."

— Mark Twain "Life on the Mississippi," 1883

Even in 1883, the Chicago that Mark Twain loved was already a remarkable Midwestern city, poised to become one of the greatest cities in the world; but, nothing had come easy. The Great Fire of 1871 made sure of it. The fire raged for 27 hours, killed hundreds of people, and destroyed over 17,000 buildings.

When the smoke cleared, the only surviving structures were a limestone water tower, a seminary, and three churches. Amazingly, that was enough for Chicagoans to pin their hopes on. Like the Phoenix, a new Chicago rose out of the ashes with an iron will, an unbroken spirit and the tenacity of a prize fighter.

With a rapidly growing population, Chicago soon faced another catastrophic problem. The sewage in the Chicago River, which flowed slowly through the center of Chicago into Lake Michigan, was polluting the city's drinking water. By 1900, 80,000 Chicagoans were dead from the waterborne diseases of typhoid and cholera.

To quote Mark Twain again, the city engineers "contrived and achieved a new impossibility." They reversed the flow of the river. An engineering marvel for its time, it saved thousands of lives and, more than any other single event in the city's history, secured Chicago's future.

Chicago continues to impress the world with its accomplishments. It is a city of superlatives, home of "the best," "the biggest," "the first," "the oldest," and "the tallest." Thanks to home-town benefactors such as Montgomery Ward, Marshall Field, David Rockefeller, Max Adler and John Shedd, Chicago is blessed with world-class museums, an internationally acclaimed planetarium and aquarium, magnificent public parks, and outdoor sculptures created by the world's greatest artists— Picasso, Miro, Calder, Chagall and Henry Moore.

Chicago: A Photographic Portrait introduces you to a great Midwestern city with vivid photographs of its crowning achievements along the shores of Lake Michigan and the Chicago River. It may be known as the "Second City" for its long-time rivalry with New York City, but you'll realize that there is nothing second-rate about Chicago.

Skyscraper in the Loop
181 West Madison *(opposite)*

This impressive skyscraper flaunts a classic Art Moderne style with a coating of brilliant nickel that draws the eye higher and higher to finish in a sparkle of light. At 50 stories high, it hardly makes a dent in Chicago's skyline of giants.

RiverWalk on the Chicago River
(above and opposite)

At the bottom of the stairs is a special water-front attraction enjoyed by natives and visitors. Riverwalk takes you through the heart of downtown Chicago, along the edge of the Chicago River for breathtaking panoramas of the city.

Lakeshore Recreation *(above)*

Public parks along Chicago's 30 miles of lakefront reward visitors with spectacular views of
Lake Michigan and the Chicago skyline.

Wrigley Building *(opposite)*

The Wrigley Building was constructed in 1920
as the headquarters for chewing gum magnate,
William Wrigley, Jr. Patterned after Seville
Cathedral's Giralda Tower in Spain, its gleaming
white facade consists of 250,000 individually
glazed terra cotta tiles, the most extensive use
of terra cotta in the world at that time.

Republic Statue

Hyde Park *(above)*

This is a smaller replica of the 100-foot sculpture that presided over the 1893 *World's Columbian Exposition* in Chicago and honored America's coming of age. Sculptor Daniel Chester French designed the original and the replica which honored both the 25th anniversary of the Exposition and the 100th birthday of Illinois's statehood.

Batcolumn

Harold Washington Social Security Administration Building Plaza *(opposite)*

Chicagoans love this whimsical baseball bat by sculptor Claes Oldenburg, world-renowned creator of the Pop Art Movement. Rising an imposing 100 feet, the bat is one of many monumental artworks that decorate the city's parks and plazas.

Chicago Harbor Breakwater Lighthouse

This historic lighthouse, built in 1893, was moved to its present location at the mouth of the Chicago River in 1919. A boathouse was built on one side and a structure to house the fog horn was added to the other side. Harbor sightseeing boats from the Navy Pier provide close-up views of this working lighthouse.

Chicago's Magnificent Mile *(above)*

The "Magnificent Mile" on northern Michigan
Avenue is Chicago's Champs-Elysees—a grand
boulevard with exclusive shops, museums,
restaurants and four-star hotels within walking
distance of turn-of-the-century mansions.

Millenium Park *(opposite)*

Surrounded by the Aon Tower, Prudential One
Building and other distinctive skyscrapers,
Millennium Park quickly became a popular
center for world-class art, music, architecture
and landscape design.

Reid Murdoch Building *(above)*

This 1914 landmark building is a reminder of Chicago's earlier industrial years. It is an example of a blend of the Chicago and Prairie schools of architecture, with its massive, seven-story brick facade and three-story clock tower.

The Chicago River *(opposite)*

With Lake Michigan in the background and the Marina City Towers in the foreground, this bird's eye view highlights a system of drawbridges that allows water traffic and automobiles to move smoothly around the city.

Navy Pier
Chicago's Lakeside Playground *(above and right)*

Navy Pier, a Chicago landmark since 1916, was originally designed as a shipping and recreational facility. Over time, the Pier served as a military training site during two world wars and the temporary home for the University of Illinois' Chicago campus. Today Navy Pier showcases a convention center, restaurants, shops, entertainment and exhibition facilities including Chicago Children's Museum, an IMAX theater, and the Smith Museum of Stained Glass.

Behind the statue of a hard-working sea captain, Navy Pier's amusement park beckons visitors with a variety of thrill rides, including a high-flying ferris wheel and a sparkling carousel in the romantic style of the 1920s.

Pirates at Navy Pier *(opposite)*

Captain Hook and his first mate scowl menacingly to the delight of children and adults in front of *Windy*, a 19th-century sailing ship at Navy Pier. Passengers are encouraged to help raise and trim the sails and take turns at the helm.

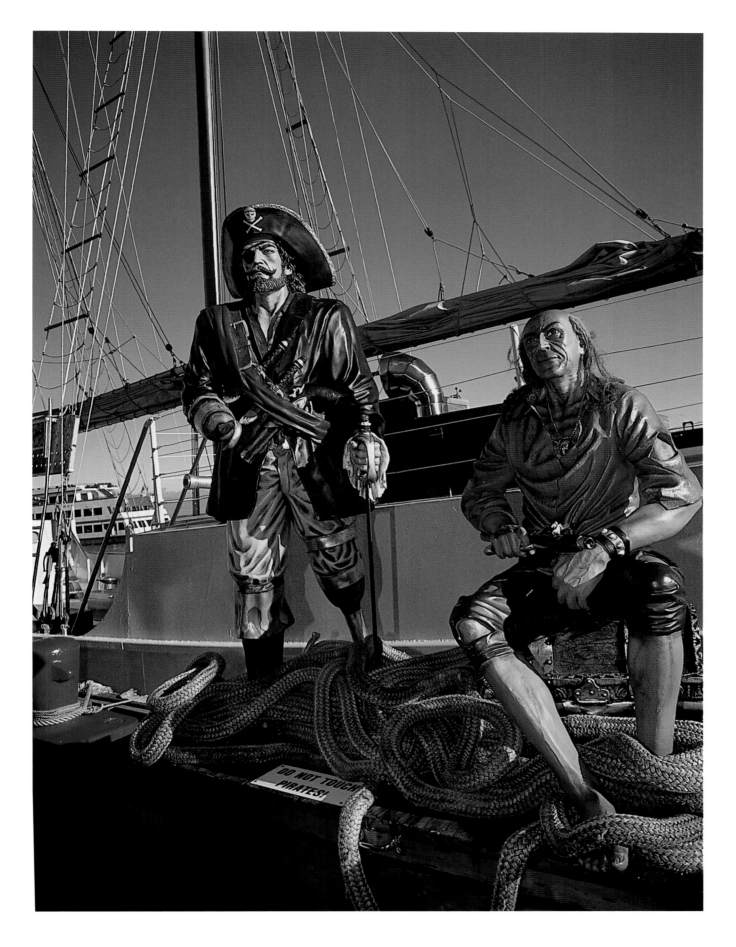

Navy Pier *(above)*

When you've had your fill of all the fun and attractions at Chicago's favorite playland, you can board the sightseeing boats that tie up along Dock Street and enjoy the Chicago skyline from Lake Michigan.

Harbor Cruises
Navy Pier *(opposite)*

Take your pick from a variety of sightseeing boats at the Navy Pier. Climb aboard *Windy* for a 19th-century sailing experience. Enjoy an elegant dinner cruise aboard the *Odyssey*. Or hold onto your hat on the 70-foot *Seadog*, one of the fastest speedboats in the country.

The "L" Train *(above)*

The colorful "L" train system has been an integral part of city life for over 100 years. Visitors to Chicago can enjoy an "elevated" journey through the city, full of great views of skyscrapers, the Chicago River, and Lake Michigan.

Pizzeria Uno *(opposite)*

In 1943, Uno's owner created the now-legendary Deep Dish Pizza. Since that time, eating pizza is Chicago has become a dining experience, not just a snack, and Pizzeria Uno and Due (right across the street) have become the most celebrated pizzerias in the world.

General Ullysses S. Grant Memorial

Lincoln Park *(above)*

This imposing statue pays tribute to the victorious general of the Union forces during the Civil War. Lincoln Park is Chicago's main downtown park, located between Michigan Avenue and Lake Michigan.

Museum of Science and Industry *(above)*

This stately Beaux Arts building is home to one of the most popular museums in the country. Its 800 exhibits include an actual WW II German submarine, the Apollo 8 Command Module—the first manned spacecraft to orbit the moon.

Waterfowl Lagoon
Lincoln Park Zoo *(above)*

Behind the scenes of this pristine habitat is a
serious conservation program that has enjoyed
tremendous successes, including the 2002
release of rare Trumpeter swans back into the
wild after being bred and raised at the zoo.
The largest waterfowl native to North
America, the Trumpeter swan was nearly
extinct by 1930.

Grant Park and Skyscrapers
Prudential One, Two and Aon Towers *(opposite)*

Beyond the small fountain in the foreground is
a teasing glimpse of Grant Park's magnificent
Buckingham Fountain (see page 56). Nearby
Chicago's famous buildings shimmer under a
clear, blue sky.

Pier Walk Sculpture
Navy Pier *(above and left)*

Every year at Chicago's popular Navy Pier, visitors come to experience *Pier Walk*, the biggest exhibition of large-scale sculpture in the world. The 2004 Pier Walk featured dozens of provocative pieces by international artists. A two-headed rubber ducky and a barrel-bodied pig were among the animal sculptures that amused and delighted visitors, young and old.

Art Institute of Chicago *(opposite)*

The Institute was founded in 1879 as both a museum and school and was re-built on its present site after the 1871 Chicago fire. Today the art museum houses one of the world's finest collections, encompassing over 5,000 years of artistic expression from cultures around the world. The school's graduate program is continually ranked as one of the best in the country.

Fountain of Time Sculpture
Washington Park *(above)*

The massive, concrete fountain by renowned
Chicago sculptor Lorado Taft, was dedicated in
1922 as a tribute to 100 years of peace
between the United States and Canada and
depicts Father Time watching over a proces-
sion of 100 human figures.

Marina City Towers *(opposite)*

Nicknamed "the Corncobs," there are very few
buildings in a city's skyline that are as instantly
recognizable as these scalloped twin towers on
Chicago's riverfront.

The George Washington-Robert Morris-Hyam Salomon Memorial *(above)*

One of the few monuments honoring non-military personnel, this statue, on Chicago's River Walk, shows General George Washington clasping hands with civilian supporters, Robert Morris (left) and Hyam Salomon (not shown). Both businessmen helped raise thousands of dollars to finance the Revolutionary War.

Marina City Towers *(opposite)*

When architect and Chicago native Bertrand Goldberg conceived Marina City Towers in the 1960s, he was not just erecting apartment buildings, he was designing a self-contained "city within a city" to help stem the urban exodus to the suburbs. Today the Towers are experiencing a "renaissance" and, as always, the view is fantastic from every apartment.

China Town Shopping Center *(above)*

In the early morning quiet, it is hard to imagine that this China Town shopping center will soon bustle with activity as merchants open their stores and shoppers come to buy everything from herbal medicines and oriental spices to silk slippers and jade jewelry.

China Town Sign *(right)*

Chicago's China Town is one of America's largest Chinese communities. Visitors are welcomed with a sensory feast of oriental music, brightly colored wares and aromatic promises of Cantonese and Szechuan delights.

Fountain of the Great Lakes
Art Institute of Chicago *(opposite)*

The five female figures that adorn this famous fountain by Illinois native Lorado Taft symbolize the five Great Lakes. The graceful figures are grouped together so that water flows from their shells in the same way it passes through the Great Lake system.

35

China Pagodas *(above)*

These red pagodas are a picturesque place to rest and enjoy the unique sights and sounds of Chinatown. In China, during the first millennium, beautiful pagodas were built near temples and on hilltops to protect towns from floods and to placate the spirits of nature.

Osaka Garden

Hyde Park *(above)*

Osaka Garden began when Japan built a replica of a famous Japanese pavilion at Jackson Park's Wooded Island for the 1893 Chicago World's Fair. It was destroyed by fire, but gardens continued to expand it into this tranquil retreat.

Cloudgate Sculpture
Millenium Park *(above)*

British sculptor Anish Kapoor created a monumental piece of art for the new Millennium Park. *Cloud Gate*, nicknamed *"The Bean,"* is meant to resemble a drop of liquid mercury hovering at the point of landing on the plaza.

Chicago Water Tower *(opposite)*

Built in 1869 this limestone Gothic-style Water Tower survived the Great Fire of 1871. Inside, a spiral staircase wraps around a long-gone water pipe. Designed more like a European castle than a municipal building, this landmark building today houses photography exhibitions.

Aon Centr *(above)*

Chicago's Millennium Park is surrounded by some of the city's tallest buildings. In the center is the 83-story Aon building, which was the world's fourth tallest building at its completion. The distinctive, triangular cap of the 64-story Two Prudential Plaza can be seen to the left.

Chicago River *(opposite)*

The Chicago River plays a leading role in the city's history. In 1900, the river's current was permanently reversed to flow away from Lake Michigan to end drinking water contamination that killed over 80,000 in the 1880s. The reversal is credited for Chicago's very existance.

Smurfit-Stone Building *(above)*

The gleaming white exterior of the Smurfit-
Stone building is accented with dark stripes of
windows rising up to a diamond-shaped top
that slants toward Lake Michigan. This whimsical effect makes it appear to be growing, like a
massive lily sprouting on the lakeshore.

Pritzker Pavillion *(opposite)*

A main attraction of Millennium Park, the
Pavilion's extraordinary band shell design was
created by world-renowned architect Frank
Gehry. Its massive panels of stainless steel
resemble the graceful blooming of a flower or
the unfurling sails of a massive ship.

Batcolumn Sculpture *(opposite)*

A creative camera angle transforms this 100-foot-tall pop art sculpture of a baseball bat into a whimsical Chicago skyscraper. The Swedish-born sculptor, Claes Oldenburg, grew up in Chicago.

Chicago Skyline *(above)*

Chicago's eclectic skyline shimmers under blue skies, while, in the distance, clouds gather low over Lake Michigan.

Rockefeller Memorial Chapel
University of Chicago *(above)*

In 1910, John D. Rockefeller requested a striking chapel be built as the central feature of the
University. Today the limestone chapel's Gothic
lines grace the campus, and the craftsmanship
of its interior inspires awe and reverence.

University of Chicago Campus *(opposite)*

Founded in 1891 by John D. Rockefeller, the
University of Chicago quickly became a national
leader in higher education and research.
Distinguished University scholars have included
73 Nobel laureates and many other recipients
of prestigious awards.

Miro's "Chicago"
Brunswick Plaza *(above)*

Spanish artist and sculptor Joan Miro created
this 40-foot-tall abstract of a woman with out-
stretched arms. Chicago is known for its monumental abstract art by the world's masters.

Union Station's Great Hall *(opposite)*

The Great Hall of magnificent Union Station
showcases the drama of Beaux Arts architecture. With 114-foot vaulted skylights, marble
floors and Corinthian columns, this is one of
the last, grand railway stations in the country.

Chicago Yacht Club *(above)*

In 1869, eight sailors with one 18-foot catboat formed the Chicago Yacht Club in an old wooden shack on Lake Michigan. Since that humble beginning, the Club survived the Great Chicago Fire, the Depression and the city's growing pains to become, in the words of *Yachting Magazine*, "one of the country's most distinguished yacht clubs."

Grant Park

Aon Center *(opposite)*

A popular downtown park along the shores of Lake Michigan, Grant Park is a refreshing oasis where people come to shake off the stresses of the day and enjoy the beautiful scenery. The park's design is based on the popular geometric designs of French parks.

House of Blues (above)

The Blues, an American musical innovation, floated up the Mississippi River and found a welcome home in Chicago, where eager musicians perfected it and deliver sizzling performances in clubs like the original *House of Blues*.

The Chicago Theater (opposite)

When this historic theater opened in 1921, it was the largest, most lavish movie palace and stage show theater in Chicago. An architectural marvel, its design is based on the elaborate French Baroque style of the Paris Opera House.

Wrigley Field *(above, and opposite)*

Nestled in the heart of Chicago, Wrigley Field has been home to Major League Baseball's Chicago Cubs for over 90 years. Today Wrigley Field is the only original Federal League ballpark still standing. Charmingly one of baseball's most old-fashioned parks, the scoreboard is still operated by hand and there are no large ads to distract from the action on the field. Beyond the stadium walls, hopeful fans wait on Waveland Avenue to catch homeruns, while other fans sit atop buildings and cheer on their team.

Buckingham Fountain
Grant Park *(above)*

This majestic fountain is Grant Park's biggest attraction. The design is based on a royal fountain at the Palace of Versailles in France and features four pairs of bronze sea horses circling the layers of basins.

Year of the Rabbit Statue
China Town *(right)*

The Chinese Lunar New Year is the longest chronological record in history dating back to 2600 BC. The beginning of each new year varies because the calendar strictly follows the cycles of the moon. *The Year of the Rabbit* occurred in 1999 and will come again in 2011.

Tribune Towers *(opposite)*

Nicknamed "the Cathedral of Commerce," the Gothic design of the Tribune Tower pays homage to the famous Rouen Cathedral in France. The building's base contains 120 stones from locations such as the Greek Parthenon, the Egyptian Pyramids, the Taj Mahal, and the Great Wall of China.

North Branch of Chicago River *(above)*

The Chicago River's variety of 45 movable bridges represent what Chicagoans call a "city-wide museum of bridge technology." Chicago enjoys the distinction of having more bridges than any other city in the world.

Navy Pier *(opposite)*

A view of Lake Michigan from the Navy Pier gives a modest idea of the vastness of this freshwater lake, the sixth largest in the world. *Windy*, a four-masted schooner, sails into port to pick up more tourists for a 19th-century adventure on the high seas.

Lincoln Park Conservatory (above)

Built in the 1890s, the Lincoln Park
Conservatory is a tropical oasis filled with
greenery from all over the world. Outside this
popular attraction is a Shakespeare Garden,
which flourishes with 20,000 flowers and
plants mentioned in the Bard's works.

The Bates Fountain
Lincoln Park Conservatory (opposite)

This whimsical fountain greets you at the conservatory's entrance with bronze storks, fish
and small boys frolicking in the spray.

Shedd Aquarium *(above)*

Built on a peninsula on Lake Michigan, the aquarium was a gift from benefactor John G. Shedd, who wanted Chicago to have the largest aquarium in the world. Today Shedd enjoys an international reputation for its conservation programs and award-winning exhibits, featuring 750 species of fishes, reptiles, amphibians, mammals and invertebrates.

Grant Park *(opposite)*

Affectionately known as Chicago's "front yard," Grant Park is the site of three world-class museums—the Art Institute, the Field Museum of Natural History and the Shedd Aquarium.

Southshore Metra Line *(above)*

Hop aboard Chicago's commuter trains for a
quick trip to the city's lakefront, museums,
zoos, sporting events, shops and restaurants,
concerts, schools and colleges as well as
quaint, historic suburbs. Chicago's 495-mile
Metra system connects a six-county area.

Merchandise Mart *(above)*

When Marshall Field and Company built this 25-story, two-block-long building on the Chicago River in 1931, it had the largest floor area of any building in the world. Today a shopping mall occupies the first two floors and merchandising showrooms occupy the rest.

Chagall's Four Seasons Mural

(above and opposite)

Chicago's love affair with French artist Marc Chagall has been going on for many years. His massive, mosaic sculpture, *Four Seasons*, is one of Chicago's most beloved outdoor artworks. Nicknamed "the boxcar mosaic," it measures 70 feet long, 14 feet high and 10 feet wide. The glass and stone mural depicts the four seasons with fantasy characters, who cavort, dance and play music while fish and birds float about and cityscapes rise along the lower edge.

Old Chicago Stock Exchange Entrance
(above)

When the old Stock Exchange (built in 1894)
was torn down in 1972, the LaSalle Street
entrance was preserved in the East Garden of
the Art Institute of Chicago. Inside the
Institute, the Exchange's original trading room
was reconstructed with other salvaged parts.

The Harold Washington Public Library
(opposite)

The country's largest public library pays homage
to Chicago's great architectural legacy with
exterior elements derived from landmarks such
as the Marquette Building, the Art Institute, the
Auditorium Theatre and the Rookery.

Shedd Aquarium *(above)*

At night, the neo-classic, Beaux Arts lines of
the Shedd Aquarium are illuminated. Architect
Graham Anderson used ancient Greek tech-
niques to build this world-famous aquarium,
located in Chicago's Grant Park Museum
Complex on Lake Michigan.

Tiffany Dome
Cultural Center *(opposite)*

This magnificent 38-foot dome, one of two at
the Cultural Center, is thought to be the
world's largest original Tiffany dome. Valued at
an estimated $35 million, it was the first per-
manent structure of the city's public library
system, designed to be a grand civic building.

Cloud Gate Sculpture

Millenium Park *(above)*

Day or night, Cloud Gate's highly-polished
stainless-steel surface reflects the city skyline.
With a 12-foot-high concave area beneath,
British sculptor Anish Kapoor's design allows
visitors to visually interact with its mirror-like
surface.

Wrigley Building *(opposite)*

The Wrigley Building's stark white, terra-cotta
facade lights up Chicago's night sky with a
most impressive commercial lighting system.
Hundreds of thousand-watt lamps illuminate
the riverfront and street levels while dozens
more gradually illuminate the two towers.

Frank Lloyd Wright's House
and Workspace
Oak Park *(above and right)*

This is where the course of 20th-century architecture changed forever. It was here that Frank Lloyd Wright, the most important architect of his time, lived, worked, and perfected his signature "Prairie Style" architecture which emphasized the use of interior light and open spaces in low, earth-hugging buildings.

Ernest Hemmingway's Birthplace
Oak Park *(opposite)*

Novelist Ernest Hemingway was born in 1899 in Oak Park, at that time a conservative town ten miles from Chicago. One of the most important writers of the 20th century, Hemingway left his old neighborhood of "wide lawns and narrow minds" to travel the world and carve his name indelibly into the pages of American literature.

Pullman Historic District

"The World's Most Perfect Town" *(above)*

Just nine years after the 1871 Chicago Fire,
George M. Pullman, founder of the Pullman
Palace Car Company, created the first, planned
model industrial town. The 600-acre community was designed for the workers in his manu-
facturing plant. The town of Pullman thrived for
14 years until the Great Depression of
1893–94 when the economic downturn forced
Pullman to layoff many workers.

Tiffany MosaicDome
Marshall Field's Department Store *(above)*

When wealthy, dry-goods tycoon Marshall
Field built his flagship store in Chicago, he
made sure that the world's largest department
store was unmatched in elegance. The palatial
décor features this original Louis Tiffany mosaic
dome that amazes shoppers with its beauty
and warm-hued light.

Pullman Historic District (above)

With hundreds of 19th-century structures left in tact, Pullman went on to become a State, National and City Landmark District. Today the re-gentrification of Pullman is going strong as hundreds of houses continue to undergo renovation and restoration.

Gold Coast Neighborhood (opposite)

The Gold Coast is one of the city's oldest and wealthiest residential neighborhoods, rich in history, culture, and grandeur. Within walking distance of Chicago's Magnificent Mile are many turn-of-the-century mansions designed by the city's most prestigious architects.

Hotel Florence
Pullman Historic District *(above)*

At the turn of the century, when most workers
lived in shabby tenements near their factories,
the planned community of Pullman seemed
more like a dream. The former 60-room Hotel
Florence provided ornate and elegant lodging
for visitors and residents of Pullman community
and was a success from the start. In 1896,
Pullman was presented an award for the
"World's Most Perfect Town".

Union Stock Yards Gate *(above)*

This 19th-century gate, designed in 1875 by architect Daniel H. Burnham, looks deceptively like the entrance to a stately mansion. Yet, this limestone gate saw a steady flow of people and livestock for over 100 years, when Chicago was known as "the hog butcher of the world." The gate is a visual reminder of Chicago's past supremacy in livestock and meatpacking.

Notebaert Nature Museum

(above left and opposite)

Built in 1999 as an offshoot of the Chicago
Academy of Sciences, the Notebaert Nature
Museum is dedicated to education and conservation, and gives visitors a unique, hands-on
exploration of nature in the middle of Lincoln
Park. Children love this place. They can watch a
butterfly emerge from its chrysalis, squish
through wetlands, learn about the mystery of
rivers, or crinkle their noses at the "Monster
Creepy Crawlies" exhibit.

Lincoln Park Conservatory

(above right)

Amidst three acres of lush, outdoor gardens,
this world-class Conservatory displays exotic
palms, ferns, orchids and other flowering plants
inside of four glass buildings.

Lincoln Park Zoo *(above and right)*

The oldest zoo in the country is home to over 1,200 animals and is renowned for its dedication to teaching conservation and protection of wildlife. With free admisson to all, the Zoo includes two areas just for children—The Children's Zoo and The Farm at the Zoo.

Dream Lady Sculpture
Lincoln Park Zoo *(opposite)*

This charming sculpture depicts an angel watching over two sleeping children. A tribute to Eugene Field, a popular 19th-century writer of children's poems and lullabies, it is a wonder that sculptor, Edward McCarten, could have create such tenderness out of bronze.

HAVE YOU EVER

Chicago Botanic Garden *(above and opposite)*

Since 1890, generations of Chicagoans have learned about gardening from the Chicago Horticultural Society's flower shows, victory gardens, and horticultural lectures. In 1972 the Society created the Chicago Botanic Garden as a permanent site for its collections, education and research. The Garden is actually 26 gardens in one. From the romantic English Walled Garden to the wild Midwestern Prairie, specialty gardens and native habitat areas show the diversity and beauty of nature.

Sculpture at the Garden *(left)*

Sculptures throughout the 26 gardens illustrate the harmony of nature and man-made art.

Gardens of the Great Basin
Chicago Botanical Garden

Walk across this serpentine bridge to *Evening
Island*, a highlight of the Gardens of the Great
Basin and showcase example of the pioneering
style of "the New Garden." Broad swaths of
perennials and ornamental grasses combine
with distinctive trees and shrubs for a dramatic,
artistic feel.

Chicago Botanic Garden *(above and opposite)*

Paths winding over ponds, lakes, hills and meadows throughout the various "garden rooms" allow close-up views of each garden style, along with sweeping views of surrounding gardens. The Chicago Botanic Garden promotes and teaches conservation with exhibits, classes and community outreach programs.

House Designed by Frank Lloyd Wright

Oak Park *(above)*

Chicago suburb Oak Park is home to the
world's largest collection of Frank Lloyd
Wright designed buildings and houses, with 25
structures built between 1889 and 1913. Many
are now national historic landmarks. *(See
Wright's Oak Park home and workplace, page 74)*

Elks National Veterans Memorial
Lincoln Park *(above)*

Visitors to this memorial are often over-
whelmed by its classical beauty. The 1926
rotunda features elaborate murals, art-glass
windows, and bronze sculptures symbolizing
the Elks' principles of charity, justice, brotherly
love, and fidelity.

The Henry Moore Sundial Sculpture
Alder Planetarium and Astronomy Museum
(above)

Famous English sculptor Henry Moore was
commissioned by the Adler family to create
this magnificent sculpture in honor of what
was then considered "the Golden Age of
Astronomy," 1930–1980. The first major planetarium in the Western Hemisphere, it is also
the hemisphere's largest museum of astronom-
ical history. The exhibits feature over 2,000
artifacts.

Sears Tower *(opposite)*

The Sears Tower's unique design dominates the
Chicago skyline and changes shape at different
angles. Structurally, it is nine skyscrapers or
"tubes" joined together in one building to
share the lateral load and high winds that
come with being the country's tallest building.

Southshore Metra Line *(above)*

Chicago's commuter rail system makes traveling to and from downtown Chicago and its surrounding areas easy and convenient. With 228 stations, Metra serves a six-county area of northeastern Illinois.

Marshall Field's Clock *(opposite)*

A Chicago landmark, Marshall Field's Department Store, radiates luxury inside and out. Even their street clocks show the influence of the intricate design elements of the Italian Renaissance and Beaux Arts styles.

The Sitting Lincoln *(above)*

Chicago honors Abraham Lincoln, our 16th president, with five different statues around the city, including this one in Grant Park. This and the "Standing Lincoln" in Lincoln Park, both by artist Augustus Saint-Gaudens, are considered to be the best likenesses of the president.

Chicago Water Tower *(opposite)*

One of the few buildings to survive the Great Fire of 1871, the 154-foot limestone water tower became a symbol of the city's indomitable spirit of survival. It is rumored to house the ghost of a hero who lost his life manning the pumps while Chicago burned around him.

Christopher Columbus Statue

Grant Park *(above and opposite)*

The sculpted pedestal of the statue pays tribute to Columbus' accomplishments as well as those of fellow Italians, Amerigo Vespucci and Paolo Toscanelli. America was named in honor of Vespucci, who explored North and South America extensively. Toscanelli was a 15th-century astronomer and geographer who developed the iconoclastic theory that the Orient could be reached by sailing west.

Alder Planetarium *(above and opposite)*

The creation of the Adler Planetarium was a family affair. The now-famous building was designed by Max Adler's cousin, architect Ernest Grunsfeld Jr. The first structure of its kind in America, this famous 12-sided Art Deco building, with its sparkling rainbow granite façade, earned Grunsfeld a Gold Medal from the American Institute for Architecture.

The Bowman
Grant Park *(above)*

This majestic 1928 statue by sculptor Ivan
Mestrovic is one of a pair of Indian warriors at
the Congress Plaza entrance to Grant Park.
The Bowman is poised to shoot an imaginary
arrow, while The Spearman (not shown) is
shooting an imaginary spear.

Daphine Statue
Grant Park *(opposite)*

This special garden merges flowers with sculpture in a mythical tale about the Greek goddess Daphne whose father, the river god,
turned her into a laurel tree to save her from
being captured by Apollo. In the summer, flowers and vines transform her metal lattice skirts
into living sculptures.

Rosenberg Fountain
Grant Park *(above)*

The Greek goddess Hebe, cup-bearer to the gods on Mt. Olympus, adorns this 19th-century drinking fountain by artist Franz Machtl. Relatives of Joseph Rosenberg, the fountain's patron, founded *Michael Reese Hospital* and co-founded *K.A.M.*, Chicago's original Jewish congregation.

St. James Chapel
Archbishop Quigley Preparatory Seminary *(opposite)*

The design of St. James Chapel was influenced by the famous 13th-century Gothic Sainte-Chapelle Cathedral in Paris. The chapel boasts magnificent stained glass windows depicting 245 events of scriptural and Church history.

High School OPEN HOUSE
Archbishop Quigley Prep Seminary
Sat., Nov. 13, 11:00 a.m. - 2:00 p.m.
Sun., Nov. 14, 1:00 P.m. - 4:00 p.m.

Chicago Board of Trade *(above and opposite)*

The Chicago Board of Trade is the world's leading futures and options exchange. In the early years following its establishment in 1848, only agricultural commodities such as corn, wheat, oats and soybeans were traded. The sleek and stylish building was completed in 1930 and stands today as a Chicago landmark and one of the city's finest examples of Art Deco architecture. In the 1920s and 1930s, the Art Deco style became an expression of the modern world by using cubic forms, geometric ornamentation, and sleek surface materials.

U.S. Cellular Field
Formerly Comiskey Park *(above)*

American League baseball moved into this
$167-million home in 1990. Comiskey Park's
modern stadium was built across the street
from the original ballpark which was Chicago
baseball's home for 79 years. It was the first
new baseball-only stadium built in the
American League since 1973.

O'Hare International Airpost *(opposite)*

For the past several years, *Business Travelers
Magazine* has voted O'Hare International
Airport as "the world's best airport"—quite an
accomplishment considering it also rivals
Atlanta's airport as the busiest in the world.

Union Station *(above, and opposite)*

Magnificent Union Station originally consisted of two Beaux Arts buildings connected by a tunnel under Canal Street. The west building, seen here, contains the impressive Great Hall waiting room (page 48). Across the street was the glass-vaulted concourse building, later demolished to make room for office buildings. Union Station is the only passenger railway station in downtown Chicago, a reminder when Chicago was the hub of national train travel in its 1940s heyday.

The Blue Angels

Each Spring crowds gather eagerly along the shores of Lake Michigan to enjoy the nonstop thrills of the Chicago Annual Air and Water Show, the oldest and largest air and water show in the country. Two days of daredevil acrobatics climax with the ultimate crowd-pleaser—the synchronized air ballet of the U.S. Navy's Blue Angels.

Shedd Aquarium *(above)*

When Shedd Aquarium opened in 1931, it was an instant sensation, attracting millions of visitors in its first year. Today its 6,000 fishes, reptiles, amphibians, mammals and invertebrates amaze visitors in state-of-the-art exhibits such as *Oceanarium, Amazon Rising, Caribbean Coral Reef,* and *Wild Reef, Sharks at Shedd!*

Sears Tower *(opposite)*

Even though the Sears Tower is no longer the tallest building in the world, a title held for over 20 years, it still dominates Chicago's skyline and is a full 93 meters taller than the Aon Center, its closest competitor.

Chicago Yacht Club at Monroe Harbor

Chicago is a city of avid boating enthusiasts who enjoy cruising up the river or setting sails on Lake Michigan.

The Field Museum of Natural History

(above, left and opposite)

The museum is a striking example of the Beaux Arts style of architecture that was so popular in the early 1900s in America. Each detail, from the multi-story large columns across the entrance way to the smallest window ornamentation, is reminiscent of classical Greek architecture.

Magnificent Mile Shopping *(above)*

Big names have set up shop on Michigan Avenue's Magnificent Mile—from Saks Fifth Avenue and Niketown to Bloomingdales and Disney. Wide sidewalks, adorned with flower-beds, create a beautiful setting for the best shopping and dining experiences in Chicago.

Exit from the "L" Train *(above)*

When the South Side "L" opened in 1892, a *Chicago Tribune* reporter wrote that one of the system's most distinguished features was its usefulness to all citizens of the city, from "the lunch-pail crowd" to passengers "resembling gentlemen."

John Hancock Building *(above)*

Known locally as 'Big John,' the John Hancock Center is a 100-story multi-purpose building with office space, apartments, and even an ice skating rink. Residents of apartments on the higher floors sometimes find themselves above the clouds. 'Big John's observation deck gives visitors one of the best views of the city.

The Picasso *(opposite)*

Shoppers at the Farmer's Market seem oblivious to the 50-foot sculpture towering over Daly Plaza. "The Picasso," as Chicagoans call it, was a gift from the artist. Few agree on what it represents, but all agree that at 50 feet tall and 162 tons of steel, it remains a huge mystery.

Flamingo *(above)*

Staring up through the arches of Alexander
Calder's bright red, 53-foot metal sculpture, it's
as if this magnificent bird has just landed in
Federal Center Plaza. Famous for his mobiles
and stabiles, American-born Calder personally
supervised every step of construction.

Crown Fountain
Millenium Park *(opposite)*

Designed by conceptual artist Jaume Plensa,
Crown Fountain's two 50-foot towers, made of
transparent glass-block bricks, stand in the
midst of a black granite plaza covered with a
one-eighth-inch layer of water. Video screens,
set behind the glass bricks, scroll through the
faces of nearly 1000 individual Chicagoans and
showcase the diversity of the city.

Oak Street Beach from Hancock

Skyscrapers cast long shadows over Oak
Street Beach.